A Life for a Life

poems by

Steve Hallett

Finishing Line Press
Georgetown, Kentucky

A Life for a Life

ACKNOWLEDGMENTS

Thanks to the editors of the magazines in which the following poems first
appeared:

The Bitter Oleander: "Possum in the Pawpaw Tree." *Blueline*: "The Old
Forest." *Mobius: The Journal of Social Change*: "Life at Peak." *New Limestone
Review:* "Progress," and "Tree House." *Pennine Ink*: "M6." *Plainsongs*:
"Greyhound Leaving Omaha." *Roanoke Review*: "Desert Road," and "She
Remembers." *The Stillwater Review*: "Starlings."

Special thanks to family, friends, teachers, and fellow students who have
given advice, ideas, and inspiration, including Kaveh Akbar, Marianne
Boruch, Melissa Fraterrigo, Don Platt, and Shelley Tudor.

Publisher: Leah Maines
Editor: Christen Kincaid
Cover Art: Steve Hallett
Author Photo: Shelley Tudor
Cover Design: Elizabeth Maines McCleavy

Printed in the USA on acid-free paper.
Order online: www.finishinglinepress.com
            also available on amazon.com

Author inquiries and mail orders:
Finishing Line Press
P. O. Box 1626
Georgetown, Kentucky 40324
U. S. A.

Table of Contents

To Mum
thinking
of Dad

What is to Come

Take these as a snapshot,
a record of now, of this
moment, as we look out
from the peak,
down,
back into the what came before,
ahead into the what is to come.
Here shimmer
the creations
of our better angels, gutter
the spent coals of creating
too much. Astonishing
in its voltage, breathtaking
and terrible in its vitality.
Light and dark
commingling. A trail
of earnest faces, upturned,
clambers into the light
from the valley of drudgery
behind, and trudges forward,
heads bowed, backs bent,
down
into white mist
and black shadows.

Possum in the Pawpaw Tree

conjures the image of a furtive creature,
wet snout pointy pink, wide eyes glinting
from a hidden recess deep within
the droopy foliage, among scattered clusters
of plump flowers unusually hued,
burgundy, russet, nestled in the sun-stippled
shade at the margin of the forest—but, no—
that's not it at all. . .

Picture, instead, the corpse plant,
or its cousins the dead horse arum, carrion
flower, those same burgundies
you'd now call *sirloin* or *steak*, those russets,
coagulated blood, where no sugary lure
is proffered for the nectar-sipping bumble bee
or hummingbird, no treats to entice
the sweet-tooths, but scents that waft
the putrescence of death and decay—
and so the blowflies come

because the possum has been peeled
from the asphalt and hung in the tree
with a rusty wire wrapped around
its shattered hind leg, dangling,
tongue lolling from its rancid snout, eyes
oozing clot-blackened blood, a demented cloud
seething around its russet, sirloin, burgundy, steak,
coagulated blood, blackened clots, probing
into flesh, flower, flesh again, maggots
deposited into meat, flower again,
pollen shuttled from anther to pistil

so that fruits can form, fatten, ripen through
the sultry summer, so we can reach in
to pluck these strange, sweet
banana-mango-pineapple mystery things,
sit in the shade, gorge,

mouths slathered, juiced, grinning, spitting
the black seeds back into the forest.

Desert Road

Desert road, sand beneath sore feet, the horizon
curves full circle,
> great arc,
> like an ocean,
but dry, hot, lost.
Nothing moves save the wavering heat and a dust devil
in the distance who swirls himself
into nothingness.
Far-off gray-ocher mountains striated with ancient pigments,
etched by rain, scratched by wind, heat,
by the scorings and scuffings of time unbound—
the guttered remnants of a prairie
of bluestem, dropseed, coneflowers,
once undulating, amaranthine,
to the horizon, once thriving,
> ground down.
> Weather-trammeled.
I pause to speak with it but it is too old,
or I am too young. A phantom wind mutters
furtive warnings. Scattered cacti stand
like petrified traffic cops directing dust. Impassive blood-red boulders sit
in defiant congregation, lithic trolls manifested from the underworld
by the receding of the erodible earth. Prickly pears jut
from the hardscrabble like tobacco-stained teeth,
like desecrated monuments guarding the scoured gullies of the dead.
A rattlesnake eyes me
from the shade of a blistered creosote bush. I pause to look at him
but he shies away, recoils into a ball, tongue flicking from a stony grimace.
> We are not friends.
On the horizon, a plume of dust builds, approaches,
gathers around like a shroud.
> Do I need a ride?
> No.
> Am I sure?
> No.
A buzzard traces spirals above our conversation, amused.
I walk until I am.

Starlings

It's called a murmuration.
I know. Great word:
murmuration,
murmuration,
but they don't murmur,
they explode from the branches like banshees,
swoop, wheel, whirl,
a skittish black cloud that swirls
through the pale autumn sky
like liquid smoke,
yaws, plunges, divides, coalesces,
then settles back, heavy,
a prattling shadowy canopy
for the grim, divested trees.
And then they leave.
And then winter comes.

Life at Peak

What was he thinking,
the man who felled the last tree
on Rapa Nui? I imagine him hearing
the decisive crack that signals
the first tottering, the groan of resignation,
the hastening,
stepping back, stone axe hefted
onto muscled shoulder, watching limbs
shear away, the trunk crash at his feet.
What was he thinking
as this last tree finally lay flat? Did he stand there,
admiring the stump-strewn slopes, or did he shrug,
work done, walk away? —or the stonemasons
who left their glowering Moai unfinished,
embedded in the basalt walls
of the Ranu Raraku quarry—did they know
they would never finish the job?
Did they take their tools with them
as they left? Did they stop to share a drink
on the way home?

And what about the man
who laid the last stone on the pinnacle
of Temple IV at Tíkal? I imagine him standing
up there, legs akimbo, arms splayed, palms raised
to the heavens, hair streaming behind
on the rising wind of a gathering storm
like the mane of some nomadic lion, turning
full circle, scanning all horizons,
his eyes settling, last,
on a bloody sun setting.
Could he see, perched atop this improbable peak,
the jungle creeping in
to take it all back—could he have known
that this was the final denial, the last,
defiant monument of a doomed empire
soon to be lost even from memory? I imagine him

retreating back down the steps, shuffling
through the darkening village,
oddly perturbed,
to a wife, three small children, seeing them
through new eyes
as the shadows of evening lengthen.

The Old Forest

has burned—wildfire. The wind conjures
spirals of ash where nothing grows
for long, empty days
until a few clumps of mushrooms
nose out from among the charred stumps,
until a few erstwhile weeds
poke tentative cotyledons through the dust,
until the bloodroots, trilliums, columbines
summoned by the first cold spring rains return
to carpet the floor.
In time shrubs sprout,
pushing through the weeds,
and new saplings emerge, stretch,
thicken, climb, reach up
to overtop it all, spreading out high canopies
to replenish the cool, thick summer shade
of the old forest. Then fire.
Undeterred she grows back—
weeds through ash,
flowers through weeds, shrubs,
trees returning, the canopy replenished again,
and again, and again, then ice.
Not a winter's ice, but a hundred
thousand winters: an Age.
Undeterred, she trudges south—
burning, recovering, burning as she goes,
waits long years
for the thaw
then skips back north. Each weed, each shrub,
each tree, has died a million deaths,
and yet the forest,
in community, goes on.

She Remembers

She is old but she remembers
the coming and going of people.

                    She remembers
how the lively brook once staunched
beneath lines curbs and layers of tar
pounded by multitudes on a restless commute
piped channeled culverted dammed—damned—
to a retention pond a constructed wetland and
diverted downtrodden amputated
bubbled again
over age-smoothed stones.

                    She remembers
mountains scalped by grating yellow scarabs
shorelines rutted with harbors breakwaters piers
rivers dredged by barges stretched into canals
flattened with dams marshes drained
for endless lawns of corn beans wheat rice that were
resculpted by floods
reshaped by winds
restored by glaciers
renewed by the ceaseless bump and grind of continents.

                    She remembers
bacteria fungi crawling and burrowing things challenged
by Barbie dolls baseballs styrofoam peanuts batteries
paint cans fridges razor blades pesticides
wrappers and zippers and gizmos and gadgets
by a million tykes bikes trikes mics piled
as mountains landscaped even or floating
on the wide ocean or blowing in the wind
skies opaque oddly thick strangely hued billows
of darkness from oily flues water streaked
creamy frothed slicked of surface upturned fish
ocean gyre plastic island island sanctuary
of net-throttled birds a turtle choking

on a plastic bag a pelican heavy with oily goo
how with new enzymes evolved deployed
slowly munching they brought her corrupted elements back
from death
to life
from the people
new food for the trees.

                            She remembers
cities (monstrous things) loud overstuffed
that stopped crumbled were overgrown swallowed
the last survivor was a pyramid who was ground down into sand.

                            She remembers
their steps the people four palms then two feet
bare then sandaled or variously shod
and the length of them set out enfolded in earth
the feel of their passing the rapid decay of blood
organ intestine sinew then long bone and tooth
marked by a stone bearing a name
now under moss
now under lichen
now fading
now eroding
now ashes like their bones
now dust like their teeth.

Greyhound Leaving Omaha

Worms of rain wriggle down
the pane now slant onto the diagonal
now hurl themselves behind
onto the slick black
mixed into the tire-spittle
flung back as the bus pulls away
from station lights grown hazy
fading into an opaque night
a ship sailing an unruffled ocean
an ungulate grumbling across the plains
bearing the bromidic
blue-collar heart of America
on exigent voyages
to burdens unwanted or unknown
They sway like kelp on the tide
stony faces resolute
or patient
indentured to the black ribbon
They close their collective eyes
resigned determined
or defeated
moving on
moving on. . .

A Life for a Life

Is this how Tibetan peasants feel
at a sky burial as their meandering
procession shoulders a rough-hewn
wooden litter high onto a mountain crag
beneath vultures who gather in expectant circles
waiting for the body to be unwrapped
and exposed to the screeching
cold, returned to a ravenous world,
at the prattling of the birds echoing down
off impassive cliffs and bluffs, at the squabbling
over entrails, as they wend their way
silently back off the mountain?

The pine was dismissed as ill suited
to this austere Lancastrian valley.
The mountain ash made sense, namesake
of the town where he was born and raised,
after all, and a pretty tree, delicate pinnate
leaves, clusters of glossy red berries,
but not a canopy tree—a weedy colonizer
not adapted to the long haul. So the mighty
beech or oak, then, two grand old men,
and, around the kitchen table sipping
peaty memories wrung from an unfinished bottle
of Laphroaig from his treasured collection,
we decided the oak was the grander,

so his urn was upended into a soggy hole,
dust swirling out on a stiff breeze
catching on coats, in hair, brushed awkwardly
aside, or drifting on gusts up onto the windswept
moors. Roots massaged apart like the stiff
fingers of an arthritic hand splayed
into the hole, soil spaded on, a little drink
of water, and that's that. We step back
and there he lies, or, now, stands. No platitudes
to the supernatural for this man,

no lifeless stone to mark his passing,
but a living thing that says Here Is David
Hallett. A life for a life, settling into the soil,
new roots poking into his ashes,
embalming him in the moldering earth,
drawing him into the rising sap.

And how he has grown. Fifteen, now,
thickening into adolescence, knotty limbs
reaching out for their share of the sulky
northern light, roots delving deep
into the living earth, those fertile ashes
long since swallowed, seeking out
the remnants of the more recently deceased,
and he will grow on this afforesting slope
overlooking the choppy waters where the boats
sail on without his ludicrous cries
of "Lean out, you fool!" stretching out beneath
the wind-battered hills where his faded
olive jacket and ridiculous, dirty
white wool hat, perched jaunty above
a gap-toothed grin, no longer roam,

but he is there, and his leaves have scattered,
and will scatter still, rustling across
the valley floor, over the water,
onto the slopes, fickle gusts worrying
them into hidden corners among the boulders,
up onto the Dovestone or the blocky,
weathered regoliths of Indian's Head,
and the heather will absorb them, and the wild
grasses and bracken, and acorns will ripen
each autumn, squirrels thriving in their turn,
leaving their own bodies littered
by the wayside, or seized by a roving fox,
secreted away to a hidden lair to be shredded
by the urgent teeth of squirming cubs,

or a hawk will swoop down, snatch him up
and carry him over the escarpment,
this grand English oak, on and on.

Pho

It's not much more
than a pan of boiled bones,
but delicate, perfumed,
gentle on the palate.
Cilantro brings the levity,
hints of anise, citrus, cinnamon
infuse the mix. The meat is sparse
off-cuts, collateral, the extra corners
from the nether regions,
left-overs of flank, shin,
mixed-in with sinew and tripe.
So bone, scrag-ends and offal, then,
and yet a symphony—
an exalted peasant food
mastered, refined, perfected,
by the salt of the earth.

From a Knoll at Standing Rock

Astonished by the silence
of a thunderstorm
so far away across the prairie
that its bulging anvils
are shrunken to fanciful
illuminated lawn ornaments,
flashing button mushrooms
strewn across the horizon,
made unreal by the vastness—

but an anxious wind
must buffet trees there,
must press the tall grass flat.
An erratic rain
must sheet across the open country,
skittish animals stock-still, strobe-lit,
cowering beneath it, within it,
the thunder shaking the ground,
the air reverberating—
but silence.

Spellbound by this place
bigger than the imagination, awed,
disquieted, transfixed. Nothing moves
but the night.
What would I find if I turned
to look the other way?
Only the stars know.
They blink down at me
dispassionately.

Progress

Sleepy pastoral Aberpennar, nestled
in a sinuous, glacier-scooped Welsh valley blessed
with natural beauty, cursed
with underground wealth.
The collieries open,
new jobs, new arrivals, and new name:
Mountain Ash. A new town for a new Britain.

Deep Duffryn is sunk. Men are shoved
into the ground, to the seam, a quarter mile below,
to shovel out the black gold
from the black tunnels
with black faces
until the coal is gone and the collieries close
on a broken town
where only Black Lung remains—

until a phurnacite plant spawns jobs
and a toxic spew of sulfur, mercury,
wrapped in a pall of dust
making clean coal for a cleaner Britain.
But these ash mountains, this valley,
once green,
this town where the coal is cleaned,
made black.

My great-grandfather was drawn to Aberpennar to find a job in the mines.
My grandfather worked his life down Deep Duffryn to die of Black Lung.
My father, lover of nature, escaped in the night to return, years later,
botany degree in hand,
to a wasteland.

So a man was drawn to the coal
that would take the life of his son—
that would take the passion of his grandson—

what things three generations can see.

The rise and fall of an empire,
the growth and death of a town,
the promise, power, and horror of progress.

Accepting Apartheid

Lucy was unearthed here, well,
some of her, at least—enough
to teach us something about her people, our people,
the people before people. Tiny, she was,
even before she was only teeth and bone.

I stand on the roof of Africa looking out
over the high plateau from where all roads
radiate, from where humans poured out
over scrubland, desert, steppe, forest,
crossed mountain, ocean, wise—sapiens—
devisers of tools, tamed beasts, elements,
tinkered, controlled, no place resistant
to our relentless outward creep. Out from here,
so, surely, here, I can write my epic—
                              but the muse is silent.
Isn't this the poet's charge, to show
how we are, why we are, and who?
Sing, muse, sing!
But she will not—
                              and so I walk.
I see a horse.

He is stranded in a busy crossroads, filthy
hair mud-matted, ugly sore oozing yellow,
pus streaking his neck, red welts
from the yoke. Trucks blunder past
in a cacophony of diesel. Cars and put-puts
flow around him honking.
                              A broken man
begs at the curb. I fold a note
into his crumpled hand, look up to speak,
but see
he has no eyes. I'd say he was blind
but that would not say enough. This man
has no eyes. An eyeless man facing an abandoned horse,
each oblivious to the other's plight

when an image of my daughter breaks in,
primped for a show. Tudor, groomed,
all sixteen fat glossy hands of him clearing
a jump. I hear the creak of polished saddle leather,
glimpse the shining concentration in her eyes,
see his tail, trimmed and brushed, flowing
freely, her ponytail swishing.

A bus rattles past spewing a cloak of fumes.
People seep from its windows. Bundles roped
to the roof dance down the potholed road.
I turn away up a narrow alley between stick-
and-mud-walled tin-roofed shacks. Weeds
grow in corners. I skirt muddy puddles
gouged by motorcycles, mules, hand carts,
duck under lines of faded washing,
step past cooking fires where bundles of sticks
smolder beneath dinted metal pots, two women
stir a cauldron of clothes, a man tends
the strewn pieces of a dismantled bike, emerge
onto a worn-out commons—a trampled shared space.

                              I have seen frigid drizzle
seep down the impassive walls of soot-stained
mills huddled deep in soggy northern valleys,
forbidding storms grind in off the plains
grumbling, snow whipped by angry winds gather
in obstinate heaps.
                              I have collected
the passports of nations once far and foreign.
I have swum up rivers, entered bedrooms
by doors, exited by windows. I have lived, learned,
witnessed—to no avail. I know now
I know nothing.

Four bedraggled sheep browse nettles
and thistles at the corner flag, their backs

turned—but half the town must be here
lining the weedy embankment, perched
on rocks, cheering, jumping to their feet
with the rising action. A cross is met
with a sharp volley. The ball—a disfigured,
bloated marshmallow of a thing—skims
over the bar, splashes into the muddy road
spattering three men who splutter past
on one rusty motorcycle, comes to rest
beside a pile of trash where
two skinny dogs
and two skinny boys
scavenge.

I have seen babies born, emerge blue-veined,
mucus-streaked, bloodied, squeal into life
wailing, and death, his eyes opening
with the last gasp. The last gasp of my father,
to whom I said, inexplicably, It's OK Dad.
It's OK to go now, as his eyes closed
for the last time at that last gasp's end.
                              What once has been seen
cannot be unseen.

I trudge on to where the blacktop expires
and the road congeals into a grey red
ooze. A man wrestles a wooden plow
through a rock-corrupted field behind
two oxen and the evening's rain begins
to fall—African rain—it falls like daggers plunged
into the bloodied earth bent on flaying the skin
from the world, stripping the last life
from the traumatized soil. Red-ocher rivers
spring up to flush it away.

                              I have seen prairies
stretch amaranthine to the great arc

of the earth's edge, blood-red sunsets coagulate
onto scorched desert rocks, mists enshroud
the corrugated boles of giant oaks, beeches,
birches, busy beaches with ice cream, kites,
boats, bathers, sandcastles, secluded beaches
hunkered beneath rainforests dripping with moss,
fish sliding through sun-dappled water
gather in prismatic throngs around lances,
brushes, fans, brains of coral, snow ladled thick
onto the patient arms of blue green firs, moors
painted with heathery purples undulate
in gusty winds across exposed scarps. Lakes.
Canyons. Waving lawns of golden wheat…

Dusty market, furnace-like sun beating down
as if in punishment, a faceless leper approaches,
arm proffered. I wrestle coins from a pocket,
hold them out, but fear loosens my grip
and the coins fall
into the hot dust. He drops,
scrabbles at my feet to scoop them up. I walk on
three paces, four, five, glance back.
He is groveling in the dirt trying to gather
my scattered pity
with hand nubs.
And so it goes. Listen,

my son plays marimba, wields four mallets
in two slender hands, skims across the floor,
hovers over the keys like a snake charmer,
rumbles out sonorous chords rousing
the wood-paneled concert hall into sympathetic
reverberation like a sorcerer.

Down in the scorching Rift six women
materialize through the heat haze.
A mirage wavering above the blacktop

obscures their legs but I see their bony forms
manifest from the shimmer, bent forward,
a mountain of sticks perched atop each pair
of shoulders—more stick than woman—
trudging forward, dipping and rising, inching back
home to heat the stove. I watch them
straggle past until the road dips over
the opposite horizon and the mirage
swallows them whole. Do they know
they are stripping the earth of its clothes?

My son is marching with them in uniform—
high school Scarlet and Grey recently traded
for college Black and Gold—proud, in step,
drumsticks rattling out the beat, the plume
of his hat the last thing to vanish
over the edge of the world,
                                          and I am back
in my father's garden lifting fat potatoes
with a spading fork, brushing off the thick black
earth, piling abundance into a barrow. He never
said much, my Dad, but dug a hundred little holes,
filled them with sand so the carrots would grow
long, straight, true. His tomato of choice was
'Alicante', nurtured to ripeness despite the dim,
cool northern light in a greenhouse he built
onto the back of the garage,

and now camels are emerging from the mirage
in a nose-to-tail, nose-to-tail train led by men
in loose turbans shuffling forward
on worn sandals, lacerated trousers, wafting
switches to make the freight lurch on.
We watch each other as they trudge past,
each giving a small wave and nod
of understanding. The camels are overburdened
with yellow jerry-cans of water

so I understand that the men must walk
their camels back to their wives
who will soon be lighting stoves.
I wear a straw hat, a camera around my neck,
so they understand that I have a cold bottle
of water in the Landcruiser.

Like how a prairie locked into cycles of fire
burns, grows grass, grows grazers, burns,
grows grass, and weeds out the trees.
Does it envy the lush forest who stands
proud across the river
segregated by its own reinforcing cycles?

And what does the forest see?
Devastating fires
or abundant wildflowers? Grins in shanties
and frowns in palaces,
yes, I know. Miserable wealth. Simple joys,
yes, I know—priceless, free—but still.

My husband died of AIDS,

                           she says.
I'm sorry. He drove trucks for the sisal factory.
I nod. So I farm alone.

                              We walk into the fields
where the maize is long dead, shriveled,
dried to powder. She kicks over a stalk,
which shatters at the base, and stomps
it into the mud with a squelch. We look at her
bare foot, mud-caked. Drought?
The rains came late again,

                           she says,
with an upwards glance as if to accuse
some incompetent god. I nod.
I will plant sorghum next year,

                           she says,

but the sorghum is not as good.

I have seen moose wading through boreal marshes
munching garlands of water lilies that dangle
from rubbery lips dripping frigid water,
kangaroo, elk, dingo, badger, fox,
possum, snakes, elephant, rhino, a lion plunged
bloody-head-first into a zebra carcass,
Californian condors, trogons, hummingbirds,
wildflowers speckling high alpine meadows,
raucous thickets of vermillion heliconias,
carpets of bluebells nodding peacefully
to the musty earth of a leaf-littered woodland.

The farmer's child lies sweating on a rough-
hewn cot in a pitiful tin shack. I give pencils
and a notebook as gifts. The farmer thanks me
as if she has received the world. The child
stares blankly at the corrugated ceiling.
Malaria,
                              she says.
I nod.
She leaves the child's side to make tea. I wait,
wafting some air onto the child's clammy face
trying not to swat at the mosquitoes
who whine about my head, because, I think, somehow,
that might seem insensitive,
                              and drift back
to the time I tripped on mefloquine, rabid dogs
snapping foam-stuffed maws, turtle-sized
cockroaches crawling up onto the bed,
waking panicked beneath a mosquito net,
wide-eyed, sweat-slicked, shaking,
gradually clearing out the hallucinations, realizing
my mistake. That was the night
I thought there was nothing in the world worse
than antimalaria pills—do not take with alcohol,

the label read—but, stressed and sweaty,
I could use a cold one right now.

The farmer emerges with tea and snacks.
I groan, inwardly. This is sure to give me the shits.
I'll have to remember to take my Cipro when I get back
to the hotel.
She puts the tray down beside me. I nod
in fake appreciation and eat her prized treats
through gritted teeth.

Tired, done with saving Africa, CNN blaring
on the TV at the gate, people bobbing in flimsy boats,
sick-sallow, adrift, scared, abandoned,
trekking across Europe on blistered feet toting
shock-numbed children, battered suitcases, tarps, sacks,
blocked at borders, stranded—
these shabby people who threaten our lifestyles.
I soar above them
heading home,
but as I look down for them
far beneath me
all I see is a rumpled gossamer of cirrus
that radiates out from here to all horizons—

and so I write.

Van Gogh's *Wheatfield with Crows*

Believing it to be his last
the eye is drawn to omens.

Death lies down each path.
Each rutted lane dwindles

through the wheat, waving,
as a murder of crows

dissembles into the sky;
until the insight is exposed

as tonypandy—a conceit—
and each saffron blade brightens,

ripples over the canvas.
A swirling wind elevates

nature to soar ecstatic
across a cobalt-phthalo sky,

bold colors compelling
the impressionist eye forward

along unexplored avenues.

Favorite Flower

Well, it's not really—
the truth is something more brassy
like a rose or lisianthus,
an orchid, perhaps,
or that insanely vivid heliconia who dongles redly
in rainforest thickets, balisier, they call it in Trinidad—
but for the sake of romance let's say
my favorite flower is henbit,
that most unassuming winter annual,
mint family,
pudgy leaves,
sparse hairs, square stems,
a tiny thing who rises barely two inches
above the ground, its inconspicuous flowers
simply too small to swoon over
(although quite lovely with a magnifying glass),
a hooded top-petal,
two lobed petals below, its fourth and fifth petals pointy
like little fangs or tusks
framing a pretty face stippled with freckles,
and all of this in a delicate purple—
but don't look closely.
That's not the idea. Don't use
a magnifying glass, no: Step back.
See that?
The winter sky is grey. A drizzle seeps from the sky.
The trees, leaves long lost, are barren—all gnarly
fingers and knuckles. The world has lapsed
into quiescence, and then
the henbit.
The fallow fields blaze.

Out of Africa

Some came from The Gorge
to Old Mali
and the Kamby Bolongo.
Others trod north through the gap,
clambering over Caucasians, Carpathians,
or settled on the steppe
until driven out by some madman.
Still more risked the Back Way.
Long ago Moor melded into Andalusian,
Gitano, became conquistador.

Immigrants out of Africa
painted Lascaux, Chauvet, Altamira,
joined the legions of world shakers
riding elephants into Rome.

Others turned right, stole into Jerusalem,
settled Eden, Mohenjo Daro,
the Middle Kingdom, Agkor,
or sailed from island to island to island,
or crossed the frozen straits
scaled mountains, traversed the howling plains,
deserts, furious with heat,
the Isthmus of Darien, the fevered jungle,
down
to the tip of the world.

Sons and daughters of Africans:
did we travel too long,
too far? Did we lose ourselves
along the way?

And still we come—
or, now, *they* come—
along those same trails trampled flat,
trodden and retrodden,
no longer striding fearful yet undaunted

into a vast unknown, intrepid, eager,
but daunted,
fateful,
knowing, now, barriers.

Oldham, Lancs.

There is a reason they brought the looms here—
it rains. It rains
like a steady penance. Moss grows in crevices
on sop-glazed red brick walls
and when the rain naps puddles linger
beneath skies grey or greyer, thickets of nettles and thistles
crowd embankments, ginnels,
cluster thickly along rot-warped fences.
What comes here skulks-in off the Irish Sea
to cower beneath the raw edge
of the shuddersome moors. What is born here
must leave to learn
not all the world is slate.
Where better to spin un-frayed cotton
than this glowering dank?—

but how those first immigrants must have felt,
dun rain jackets tarpaulined over
irridescent salwar kameez,
churidar stuffed into brown boots,
clomping to the mills in the winter evening darkness,
the incessant rain, returning
in the winter morning darkness,
the incessant rain, from the inglorious night shift
spurned by the locals.

Leaving here was easy—
a simple toddling away from the crib,
crawling out from beneath
the terraced rows, the musty old school,
nothing more natural
than stepping beyond
to where a warming sun might shine,
to where a warming wind might rustle dry—
but coming home—
coming home—the center has shifted. This place
from which all else once radiated,

against which everything was once compared,
now pushed to the periphery,
an outpost,
peculiar to me.

The mills closed years ago, and yet
the immigrants' childrens' children clomp on,
dun rain jackets tarpaulined over
irridescent salwar kameez,
churidar stuffed into brown boots,
even as the racists skulk-in to gather
beneath the raw edge
of the shuddersome moors.

On Time

Time past time present time future
might flow like a river
along an inflexible path

but watch with your mind's eye
some old man back bowed legs buckled
cane gripped in a gnarly fist peering
out through the window contemplating
the garden or gazing beyond the trees

How did it pass so quickly?
And how little remains

A grandchild scampers into his picture
chasing a terrier (or a cat if you prefer)
whiling it away wasting it so freely
in skips and smiles
impatient
to spur it faster forward

His gaze turns to the linden tree
her bole thick and fluted her hoary limbs
arched down to the ground
He remembers the planting
those present now passed

and beyond the tree he sees
the buttressed mountain rise
heaving up from the earth's crust
whipped by winds whittled by rain and snow
crags ridges bluffs scoured
by its eternal cut and thrust

and beyond the mountain the sky
the stars
it arcs around them
dancing with the light dancing with gravity itself

He watches it spiral among galaxies
plunging swooping converging

to waltz him through the cosmos
with his people.

Tree House

I freed the old linden tree
from his shackles today—
sloughed the boards
from his outstretched limbs.
Grown, left,
or soon leaving,
they no longer climb
up his knotty trunk
or out onto his broad shoulders.
Sap wept
as I drew out the carriage bolts.
Sadness?
The pain of excision?
A sudden gush of relief, perhaps,
that through all those games
on perilous heights,
none of them fell.
A single defiant bolt
remains
entombed in his wood.

Sunday Morning

I have awoken early to stillness,
made coffee,
stretched out on the sofa
beside Max, to read
beneath the wide window
where the first feeble light
lets in. Fat snowflakes fall soft
through the grey
to smooth out the irregular contours
of the shrubs. The last tendrils of night
rise out of the grass,
unravel from the trees,
lift away in invisible mists—silence
save the gentlest ruffle
of turning pages
and the sleepy
sighs of the dog—peace, indeed.
I tiptoe to the bedroom,
peek in, and see you splayed
out, under, over,
coiled in the covers
like some tornado survivor
mumbling secret invocations
to you own perfect morning.

Dreams

are trees
lying still
across the water,
sparse tops scratching
your toes,
fluted columns
rooted
into the distant bank.
Clouds of white
swans pass
silently through.
A mist of midges
fusses
among the branches
until a fish
rises,
ripples the surface,
and sends you
into morning.

African Roads

No matter how far out in the middle of nowhere
you may seem to be,
far removed from the nearest village or town,
people will be walking
along the side of the road.

It may curve along the turbid river's banks,
wind through thorn bushes,
cut across the dusty valley bottom,
but people will be walking—
and none travels unburdened.

Women walk straight-necked balancing bundles
on their heads—pots, pans, buckets—
or bent forward, a mountain of sticks
perched on their necks.
Men tote tattered sacks bursting with charcoal
stitched together with twine,
or gravitate toward distant plots,
a mattock or shovel hefted over a steady shoulder.

Even squadrons of children trudge steadfastly
from here to there
on some mysterious errand,
eyes fixed on the far horizon,
heads up,
bare feet bound to the weathered red dust
practicing the long, patient strides
these African roads demand.

Sacrifice

The bamboo pole flexes
and groans
under the awful burden
of two rough wicker baskets stacked
with gnarl-fingered hands
of bananas, pock-marked mangoes,
stretched thin
by precarious dunes of wilt-wrinkled
oranges that gouge into her shoulder.
Stooped.
Crumpled by the weight.
Scoured craggy—like stone whittled
by wind-driven sands—
grimacing yet determined
she staggers on,
each stuttering step securing a little more,
something better than this—
a pair of Levi's
perhaps—
for her oblivious grandkids.

The Birds and the Bees

What sensation does she feel
that causes her to arch back
just so
as he brushes aside petals
into pistil, nosing into her
membranous corolla—
as he waggles urgently
to drive deeper, seeking out
the sweetness within? She curls
into herself to touch her stigma,
glistening,
against his abdomen, reaches in,
filaments grasping,
to receive his precious dust,
knowing hers is not the only nectary
he will taste today. He squirms off,
lifts his weight away,
and she relaxes, flexes back,
nodding, nodding, while,

in the next bed, tendrils clasp
the leathery skin
of a thick mahogany, twine around
its stiff branches. Extensile pedicels jut,
flaunting neon red flowers
that flare about
a cushiony labellum, eager
to catch the eye
of some flighty suitor—
and here he comes, feathers
shining iridescent, wings flashing.
He hovers, alights, struts out
onto her turgid operculum,
kneels, reaches in,
proboscis probing until, his payment
of pollen made,
he streaks furtively back

into the shadows

while the gangly grasses look on,
doleful voyeurs that they are,
their diminutive green-grey
anthers drooping
from dehiscent panicles,
their wrinkled, papery packages
tossed out into the desperate
void carried by nothing
but the empty air. They stretch
on in drab monotone as the birds
and the bees pass by, indifferent—
but what is that sound?
Why do the grasses sigh
just so
as the wind strokes gently
across the plains?

The Wisdom of Plants

They neither run nor hide, but stand,
impassive stitches
in the silent green cloak of the Earth
who live the long, patient generations
of the eaten—

but they do react, my love, they do
respond—behave—smell, see, feel, stretch out
into the rising morning, unfurl,
curl up, huddle together for warmth,
tendrils grasping.

A seed lies dormant, clasped in cold, watches,
ignores the frigid rains of winter, awaits
the sun's steady climb, unlatches
at the drizzling-in of the equinox, arises
from quiescence, sends radicles probing down,
plumules reaching skyward.

No acts of whimsy, or thoughts, eager or rash,
neither imagination nor intuition guide them,
but the solutions of the infinite
interrogations of nature—
listen,
and you will hear them calling:

A pale leaf is begging for nitrogen.
A gaudy flower beckons a lover—
proffers sugar. The grass entices the grazers
to prune it back
and tear up the encroaching trees.

London Fog

Who can say where it begins, or began,
or when—high on this frost-crusted plateau
at the roof of the world, perhaps,
where a small boy, thickly clad, wafts a bent stick
to steer his animals down a hardscrabble slope
to a boggy depression among the pebbles.
Water has seeped under snow and stone
to gather here. The animals bow their heads
to suck moisture from hoofprints pressed
in the wearied ground. The boy sits on a rock
backlit by an opalescent sun
who glances in through the high, thin air,
witnessing this first flow.
He cannot conceive of where this water has been,
where it will go, or what it will do
as it percolates down its predestined path
following each inevitable turn
through beds of sand,
along cracks and fissures,
winding along its serpentine trail.

The trickle finds friends saturating their own
beds of sand, oozing from their own
pebbles, seeking their own channels,
and jostles with them at the edge of the high col
as trickle begets trickle
and rivulet begets rivulet,

and the animals and the boy recede. Nomads
they may be, but they know nothing
of the epic journey at their feet. Their destiny
is to stay while the water moves on.

Thin films gather, secretively, to coalesce
beneath a fragile crust of ice,
score out a haphazard pool,
swirl awhile,

stumble
    over a meager step
    as if poured from a jug,
curl tentative eddies, and seek out
the long, wide curve of the plateau's edge,

where a woman in a thick woolen chuba
scoops water with a metal can. Three small children
squawk like chickens, wriggling in her grip
as she catches them, one by one, and washes their faces
with the frigid water. She looks out
over endless corrugations to where
the teeming plains thrum with imagined ardor
and a coy sun blushes.

The stream forges on in translucent ribbons
mustering a small, gurgling rundle among boulders
before wheeling around the bend to peer over the edge—
a rollercoaster teetering
at the lip of the first big drop,
riders agape,
gathering,
swooping out and down, free-
falling,
shearing
into curtains, fragmenting into drops,
shattering into spray, spume, a mist rising up
off the surface, prismatic in the sharpening light.
It rushes   in   waves   and   rolls,
smashes over rocky cataracts,
                          sweeps around a wide curve,
punches through a buttressed canyon
to crash over another heady free-
fall,
bursting
into foam as it plunges
down the mountain.

It settles awhile to gurgle through a high forest
shrouded in mist. Snow lingers
in shaded crevices.
A kingfisher sits patiently
on a mossy branch watching fish slide
through the water like flecks in polished jade.
Perhaps deer browse around some hidden
corner breathing steam into the raw air.
Perhaps a snow leopard, hunched low,
is stalking them, silently placing soft paws,

but now comes a second river as potent
as the first. The two meet around the elbow
of a craggy hill crashing into each other
like ebullient friends spinning into a boisterous
embrace that spawns whirlpools and befuddled waves
that leap, swirl, chatter, then settle
into the new rhythm of their combined surge
and pour into the peopled lands

where multitudes gather in its thrall,
steer sampans across its determined spate, leap across
on bridges, throw nets, drop lines,
		where a first dam looms
		holding back a still lake
drawing it through deep tubes and turbines,
spitting it back, foaming,
and dam follows dam as the river descends
by steps
toward the plain.

Streams hurry out of the foothills, waterfalls
spill into the current, and the spreading flow
sluices into an expanding valley.

Barges of grain, coal, and steel groan
in hectic quays. A ferry sputters

toward the far bank spewing a thunderhead
of black smoke. A young woman clings
to a railing, looks down, contemplates
the churning depths below.
An old man flicks a spent cigarette into the water,
casually lights another. Vehicles splash
through oily streets. Rain washes their discharge
down slimy gutters. A factory excretes.
A million toilets flush.

The river shudders but glides on, thick
and black, as the horns and sirens recede.

A heron floats aloft on arched wings
peering down, watching the water
effuse onto the flatlands in an indolent flood.
Bamboo enclosures pattern the expanse,
nets and traps ensnare fish and crabs,
channels and ditches spread turbid waters
onto saturated paddies where men
wrestle oxen through congealed muck
and women in triangular straw hats bend
in wavy lines among emerald rows. The water
stains their ankles red-ocher as it bleeds
across the sodden landscape.

It tastes the salt,
senses the ebb and flow of the tides, splits,
divides, fans out onto the marshy flats.
It has slowed,
spread wide,
                    and stalled.

The last remnants of its silty burden fall.

Mangroves sprout on miniature islands
and embankments, their muddy feet

patrolled by determined posses
of fiddler crabs.

It seeps in a hot sheet out onto the cold salt,
is mingled back into the chasmal deeps,
home,
it rests.

Cold.
Dark.
Silent.
Still,

until raised back into the gyre to circle
the yawning expanse and loop the notch
between continents, until hoisted back over land,
goaded high into the anvil of a snow-heavy cloud,
and loosed to fall.

Centuries in ice scooping out a wide mountain valley.

A cornfield . . .

Humidity

Three in the morning,
noodle soup, warm beer,
Saigon presses-
in around me,
strained,
thrumming
with the silence of an over-
stretched violin string,
taut,
but as-yet un-
plucked. Even the air is
anxious,
overburdened with a hot damp that
quivers
between cumulation and release—
tensed
to be loosed.
Tropical cities at night
seethe
with restless impatience.

Let it Be

Let the oceans rise
Let the forests burn
Let the glaciers melt
      and the icecaps
Let the rivers flood
      or run dry
Let the deserts advance
      trampling burying
      hapless abandoned outposts
Let the crops wither
      and curl up
      laying dusty in the fields
Let the cities drown
      or scorch
Let the people flee
      hot scattering desperate
      to escape your wrath then
Let them broil
      in the humid heat
      that settles on the parched plains
Let them roast
      in their self-made oven
Let this culture curse
      its deservèd fate and
Let their bleached bones
      be scattered
      along the path
      of least resistance.

The Crossroads of America

Once it was.

Here is where the imperforate
woodlands met the boundless
prairie, where wildlife thrummed
in vast wetlands,
birds flocked
on epic migrations,
where a dozen tribes hunted
bison and deer,
gathered berries and wild rice.

Now? Now it is
brown,

                with precious flecks of

green,
white,

                with precious flecks of

black,
red,

                with precious flecks of

blue,

and vapor trails crisscross the sky.

Adieu

So here we are at the end of things,
your coffin disappearing into a hole
clean-cut by a rusty yellow excavator
that waits around the corner
to backfill you into the sodden ground.
The priest is mumbling practiced incantations
unheard over the static
that crackles through the cosmos.

Black-clad mourners stand sullen
beneath a cheap canvas canopy
a respectful distance from the dizzying fall.
A motor strains in complaint
as it lowers you, stutteringly,
into the darkness.

I see him stoop—the vicar, or priest,
or minister, or whatever he is—
to toss dirt onto your varnished wooden lid.
Ashes to ashes, he says, dust to dust,
and the worms are awakening.
The bacteria and fungi, too,
are stirring in the soil, creeping into the wood,

while already on the inside, those microbes
who once digested your lettuce and spinach
are digesting you;
bloating your viscera, creeping from crevice to crevice.
Bones in a year. In a century only teeth.
Absorbing you into the earth entire,

but the earth spins on.
The great glaciers will return to scoop you up
and scrape you south,
and the continents will grind and moan, plate over plate,
and drop you down on some new island
lapped by some new sea,

and the reddening sun will swell and swallow us all
until you are beside me, again,
shining your light across the universe.

Misty Morning, February

One of those strange winter days,
the snow melted
in a spate of not-so-cold
that has left the ground frozen
beneath a slimy surface.
All is silent
as if paralyzed.
The trees, long leafless,
knuckles bared,
point their twisted fingers skyward
in admonition.
No shadow separates
where the grey trees meet
the grey sky.
No shadow separates
where the grey trees meet
the ground.
A thin, stagnant mist thickens
as the trees exhale.

War Museum, Saigon

I sit on the steps outside, horrified
by what I have just seen.
Unspeakable guilt. Obscene
imperial power loosed, vile
abuse, images of monstrous disfigurement,
malformation,
inconsolable mothers surviving
murdered children, the limbless,
the shattered, and on,
and on.

An old man settles beside me,
drops his chin to his chest,
clasps wrinkled hands onto his lap,
watches his feet
for long minutes
then turns to look at me, his face
impassive save a single tear
that streaks his cheek. His eyes
peer into mine—
through them—
holding my gaze with a thousand unspoken questions,
and then he nods, gently,
four times.
His eyes soften, he nods
twice more.
The corners of his mouth flinch
as he stands to leave.

I watch him hobble
down into the courtyard,
pass the massed ranks of fighters,
bombers, tanks, field guns
without a glance, and shuffle
toward the gates. I expect him
to turn back
to look at me, to wave, perhaps,

or nod, or smile—I don't know why.
He doesn't, of course,
but simply steps out into the seething city
where the crowd
swallows him
like a ripe fruit.

This Snowflake

The flurry has blown on
the night a dense indigo
now still
but one last snowflake
is still tumbling
end over end
spiraling down drifting
dancing alone through the lamp light.

Born in a high cold cloud
a thin sheen of ice on spore
on pollen or on speck of dust
a microscopic jewel
tiny
that falls and grows
crystal upon crystal finger
upon finger limb
upon limb
as it drifts along its path.

What chance that it will return
one day this snowflake
this singular flourish
of nature's art
of water's most dazzling finery
floating free
glittering for an instant
in burnished perfection
once it lands softens melts
darkens
and is poured back into the mix?

Wetland

A pipe has broken.

Water gushes
down the street,

surges down gutters,
floods over leaf-choked grids,

over curbs, sluicing
through the iron gates

to flee into the small park
at the corner of fifth and main.

It soaks into
the flower beds.

The lawns
are a pond,

the playground
an archipelago,

red slide, blue teeter-
totter, yellow swing set

cast adrift
amid ruffled waters

where ducks now swim
among the colored poles.

Summertime in the Garden

I shoo a chicken
from my age-peeled Adirondack chair
to settle beneath the smothering limbs
of the old beech tree
and recline in the shade.

A sulky breeze perturbs
clasping mantles of leaves. Sunlight stipples
blotched shadows. Tomato vines push against
the greenhouse glass
like verdigris prisoners. I'd hear them cry out
but for the urgent rustling of leaves
making sugar. Onions align
like wilted soldiers trudging taciturn
back from the front in khaki and olive green.

The chickens squabble
as they sift through leaves
in the hunt for bugs. A cicada
springs up, buzzes away
to escape a first sharp beak,
flops down near a second,
and is snapped-up whole.

A warning squawk, and the chickens scuttle
under the tree—a hawk circles overhead,
banking around and back,
drifting through the blue,
an aerial shadow cast
each time his red tail passes
across the sun. He folds back wings,
drops, swoops.
Baby rabbit breaks from the cabbage patch,
dashes out onto the lawn,
is pinned.
A talon pierces the heart. A beak pierces the skull.
Little bunny is lifted up, away,

and the chickens return to the lawn.
I sit in the shade of the old beech tree,
at peace,
admiring summertime in the garden.

Return to Aberdovey

I see you in the headland.
A sullen grey cloud settles
in the small of your back
as you lie sleeping,
stretched out across the bay
where the reckless waves crash.

I hear you in the wind
whispering invitations
and eerie incantations
like some impish siren
luring lovelorn sailors
down into the deeps.

I smell you in the mist
that carries musty scents,
seashells, driftwood stranded
moldering above the tideline,
battered seaweed
that writhes on the rocks.

I feel you in the sand
that nuzzles between my toes,
clings to my sole
with each stuttering step
like the defiant limpets
who grip the rocky shore.

I taste you in the salt
when the impulsive squall rises,
whips spray off the water
to my lips, my skin,
soaking in through every pore,
entombing me in you.

Window Seat, Rainy Day

Tucked behind glass, watching
an aquarium of humanity meander
among petrified towers
like smoke seeping through trees.
The streets are the voids between worlds.

A turtle snaps up squid
from the impenetrable black depths
from which all comes.
To which all returns.

A dandelion beckons a bumblebee.
Are the trees' rustlings stilled
by the death of the wind, or killed
by frost and fall? Be quiet and listen:

A smile shatters doubt like glass.
The mouths of new lovers ache
with anticipation. A dancer is seized
at the leap's apex, waits an eternity
for the awkward thud of landing.

Sparks float into the night sky, mingle
with infinite vacuums bombarded
by a billion explosions. Leaves unfurl,
grasp at the sun. What sound
do the worms make, I wonder,
as they nose their way through the musty earth?

A warm corner to sit—
safe to watch what passes—until you stop
in the rain, turn,
and peer between the worms of rain splayed
on the glass like question marks.
Why aren't you swimming?

People-Watching

You have been called cold
You have been called trivial selfish heartless perhaps
but only by those who see only surfaces catch only glimpses
neglect to look beneath
fail

as I will fail now
looking out from my introvert's corner

at how strangely people move
the projection of self-image in their gait
doubtful shuffle awkward lope
self-conscious stride practiced step

at how they grin giggle smile politely
or warily eyes blank grimacing
or flash a furtive glance at one they should not
eyes suddenly brighter in a shared moment
secret
but for me spying

how they laugh openly or guarded
carefree or careful
how they stand together apart
angled in angled away
flirting here attraction veiled there disdain
stiff or nonchalant or anxious

Watching strangers
feeling clever at first but slowly seeing less with each watching
knowing less
finally ceasing to judge discovering
we are each of us
haunted

Sometimes animated
Sometimes paralyzed

and then I see you in the quiet shadows across the room
watching me
Your half smile makes me shiver
Your eyes
vaporize the room.

Permanence

How the light refracts through
the pristine water, luminous curves dance
on the sandy bottom, flash
like twirling skirts, glinting
fringes and ruffles pirouette
across a wide fan, gilt-edged, a bulbous cushion
shaped like a swollen brain, a giant clam,
green-frilled mouth agape,
now a thicket of antlers
whose brown fingers, yellow-nailed,
jab at the sky.
              Tiny mouths poke
from the very living rock
stirring spirals of food, daubing
calcium to build their homes,
layer upon layer
      upon layer.
See the fish:
              What reckless abundance!
They nibble at polyps,
peep coyly from behind
a sponge. Watch a multitude
on the move: a synchronized shoal
of silver sides shining, a hundred
thousand spinning mirrors.
A squadron of cuttlefish morphs,
shape-shifts, iridescent
as it meanders by. The razor-lined maw
of a moray smiles from a rocky alcove.
Now a crimson-emerald angel hovers
beside stony-grey pillars.
Now a clown flaunts his hot
orange stripes perusing anemones
who flop from side to side,
drunkards in the pulsating waves
that sweep across
these sculpted limestone fissures and channels.

My breathing echoes in my mask.
My blood pulses.
I suck air from my world, above,
and my head is a cavern,

which draws me underground
to some distant future. Still here,
still in this place, but the fish
are gone. Deep in the earth, now, standing
in a cave, ghostly, like some haunted
travertine womb,
breathing clean, cold air. Water drips
all around. This water has dripped
for a hundred thousand years.
One precious droplet coalesces at the tip
of a stone dagger catching the light,
       blue, green, sparkling
       in suspended animation,
       a miniature world entire.
Suddenly, loosed to fall, it splashes
down to an emergent spire who reaches up
to make the catch. The light is prismatic
in ribbons of wet rock
striped yellow,
       ocher, orange, red.
A tiny waterfall. Thin curtains of water
dribble over lace-pattered curtains
of stone, drip
from sculpted limestone fissures and channels
through this clandestine echo chamber,

which draws me back
here—and now—rebounded,
blinking, breathless, remembering
where I am and when. I emerge
from my phrenic cave chilled
and exposed. The wind has risen, erratic,

fierce, buffeting up the scarp,
flowing rampant through the peaks,
      cols, cliffs, screes,
sweeping across this lithic ridge,
monstrous, like the fossilized spine
of some ancient crocodilian.
I lean into the gusts, coat flapping furiously,
eyes watering at the view—
these great, grey, erumpent mountains
crumpled by the restless, rumbling continents,
heaved up from the very living sea,
weathering,
      eroding
sculpted limestone fissures and channels,
      corrugated reefs,
of solid, unyielding permanence
that undulate to the horizon
and dissolve back
into the sea.

The Hand of the Maker

To see that painting is to see
not just the wheatfield the crows
but the hand of the artist
defying the fashion of the time
resisting the urge to reproduce faithfully
saying instead
Here I am
in these saffron scratches in these swirls
of phthalo blue in these vague Ms and Ws
which I trust you to understand
as crows lifted to soar on a gusting wind

but so too was the field
are all fields
are forests oceans prairies
riddled with imperfections parasites death decay
This tree fell
and a fledgling died
and the eggs of its siblings split open
their lumpy yokes spilled onto the leaf litter
and a parent returned early
a worm writhing in her beak
to catch sight of the hand of the maker
scratching roughly across the canvas

Microcosmos

Always one to seek meaning in things
how they are how they work
how they came to be
I suppose my god must be everywhere
or nowhere in all things
in none
in life death
or most likely in the transitions between—
present in his greatest abundance here then
in this compost pile seething
with creation and destruction—

if god is still needed that is
since we made the incredible credible
commonplace even
now that the invisible can be so clearly seen
shown so elegantly
It is microbes who sicken not demons
Hell must be in not down
Heaven not up but out
since we made the earth a sphere
What place remaining for astonishment
in the disciplined scientific mind
for wonder?

The oak tree depends on the forgetfulness
of the squirrel The hover fly's only defense
is a lie The complexity of the cosmos
inconceivable
unless—
unless you consider that compost pile
where more microbes than stars in the sky
convert a billion dead gods
into fertile soil.

Some Nights, a Little Homesick

—and the misty greys of morning begin
to lift, a paleness gathering behind
the trees as the sun sihouettes them,
now bends them, blurry

—the simplest field a dream could conjure
—with nettles—always nettles growing
in hummocks and ridges, scruffily, and docks
gone to seed, their papery stalks scattered
in clumps punctuating the foreground,
the grass shorn roughly by animals—sheep,
mostly. Cattle, rarely. No goats.
Goats would have eaten down the nettles
so there can't have been goats.
Rabbits, obviously. Sometimes I see them,
sometimes not.

—and the field is framed by oaks, beeches,
a few sycamores. That one might be a mountain ash,
but it's too far away to identify for sure—too far away
to see if it has glossy berries,
finely pinnate leaves, and yet that one,
who has stepped forward from the rest
is an oak. I'm not sure why—not sure
how I know, that is—but it's an oak—
an English oak—round, full, proud. I riddle
its canopy with squirrels: baby squirrels
racing along its knurly branches

—and the rays of a low, earnest sun diffract
into a wide fan as they glance through the uppermost
branches as the sun hesitates on its ascent

—and the grass ungreys, and the nettles regreen
in their turn

—and the dew lifts away, drawn
from the reticent ground by the rising morning.

The Snake

lies so still
on his warming rock

that those who don't know
snakes might think

he is lurking in ambush
awaiting unwary prey

skulking with ill-
intent hunting

guiltless
warm-bloods

as he scents the air
with forked tongue

feeling for movement
vibrations transmitted

through the hardscrabble
into his underbelly

He squints narrowly
through stony eyes

each twitching
branch fluttering

leaf spooking
scuttle in the dust behind

squawk above
sudden rush of air

waiting anxiously

for the sun

to slither up
over the horizon.

Petroleum Blues

Stop all the trains, cut up the tracks,
Pile all the cars in a rusty stack,
Silence the highways, and from every slum,
Roll out the wagons, let the horses come.

Stop the airplanes from circling, moaning overhead,
Let the silent sky scream the message: It Is Dead.
Put crêpe bows round the white legs of the feedlot cows,
Let oxen and horses pull rusty old plows.

It was our speed, our light, our heat and cold,
Our Barbie dolls, our stories told,
Our fries, our phones, our joy, our song;
We thought this world would last forever: we were wrong.

The pumps are not wanted now: shut off all the taps,
Dismantle the rigs and trade them for scrap,
Pack up the engines and sweep up the wood,
For none of this now can ever come to any good.

Multitudes

Hubble telescope deep field south
focused into the blackest recesses of night

where even space is empty
reveals clouds clusters spirals of light

an abundance like a stampede through the barrens
hooves pounding the Mara herds flowing

like tropical rain off a tin roof
each panicked prey isolated

solitary in the uncountable flood
We cower beneath

shrunk by its horrific enormity
reduced to fatuous gazers

reaching out to comprehend our smallness
as we cling to the thin skin of this any-old rock

Yet beneath our feet thrives another cosmos
another seethes in our gut on our skin

Ancient ones enslaved in our cells
encompass a galaxy of microbes

for whom we are the universe Shards within shards
Scattered splinters of a cosmic explosion huge as stars

tiny as atoms
who attract repel coalesce burst apart

brighten dim collapse and give birth brooding
So we?

But a mote
yet a multitude.

Raven Mill

The new, pasted and pinned to the old,
is peeling,
and the old revealed anew,
its former luster lost, to be sure—
soot-stained, moss-worn—
but still vital: defiant
in its resurrection.

The mill closed years ago,
lay dormant, empty,
then a warehouse, then a paintball arcade
whose neon lights flashed brightly,
briefly,
then guttered, rusted, flaked away in their turn
until sloughed off by the red brick palisades

to reveal that older sign—bolder—
deep-carved by those mythic giants
of industry: Raven Mill
reborn from the tattered shroud
of modern follies.
And so it still stands,
weathered but abiding,
an obdurate testament to grander times,

but yet older masters lurk. Weeds
choke the railway lines. Swallows
nest among the ramparts. Trees
poke through shattered window panes,
and the patient northern rain seeps-in,
soaks floorboards,
and bleeds down the walls.

Parent and Child, O'Hare

She lets me take her fleshy little hand
in mine, hold firmly
so I can catch her should she stumble,
grip tighter as she toddles
onto the escalator. I watch her stubby little feet
step safely over the yellow line
as the grooved steps separate,
give her a reassuring nod and smile
as we grind upward toward Departures.

We hold onto each other through the torrent
of strangers, cutting a narrow path
toward the gate. We hug at security—
I fight back tears.
She stuffs a roll of notes
into my hand, "For the children," she says,
and totters onward, boarding pass brandished
in one hand, shoes dangling
from the other, waving from beyond

the conveyors and scanners, blowing a kiss,
trampling off down the long hallway,
head up, eyes forward,
little red suitcase trailing behind.
I remain as she recedes
toward the last curve where she stops,
turns, and waves one last time—
too far from me, now, to see the tears
well-up in my eyes, but, my,
how she has grown. . .

Writing in front of the Window

head down
so long
that the day has been swallowed
by the night the light
from without lost the light
from within bounced back
The garden
has vanished the window
turned inward—a mirror
Looking up surprised to see
only myself looking back
lamp-lit alone
a solitary grey figure
where only moments ago
was the world.

Steve Hallett is a British-Australian-American poet and professor of horticulture at Purdue University, Indiana, where he studies and teaches ecology, international development, and sustainable agriculture. He directs the university's sustainable food and farming systems program and its student farm. Steve is the author of over fifty research articles and book chapters, and the author of two books: *Life without Oil: Why we Must Shift to a New Energy Future* (Prometheus Books, Amherst, NY; 2011) and *The Efficiency Trap: Finding Our Way to a New Energy Future* (Prometheus Books, Amherst, NY: 2013). Poetry is a new medium for Steve, through which he continues to explore themes of social and environmental justice, and humankind's relationship to the natural world. His poetry has been published in *Bitter Oleander, Roanoke Review, Stillwater Review, Blueline, Plainsongs,* and *New Limestone Review. A Life for a Life* is his first book of poems.

CPSIA information can be obtained
at www.ICGtesting.com
Printed in the USA
LVHW091436200120
644169LV00003B/341